FROM THE CREATORS OF FIREPROOF AND COURAGEOUS

WAR ROOM

BIBLE STUDY

STEPHEN KENDRICK ALEX KENDRICK

AS DEVELOPED WITH
NIC ALLEN

CONTENTS

ABOUT THE AUTHORS

Stephen Kendrick is a speaker, film producer, and author with a ministry passion for prayer and discipleship. He is a cowriter and producer of the movies *WAR ROOM*, *Courageous, Facing the Giants,* and *Fireproof* and cowriter of the New York Times bestsellers *The Resolution for Men* and *The Love Dare*. Stephen is an ordained minister and speaks at conferences and men's events. He attended seminary, received a communications degree from Kennesaw State University, and now serves on the board of the Fatherhood CoMission. Stephen and his wife, Jill, live in Albany, Georgia, with their six children, where they are active members of Sherwood Church.

Alex Kendrick is an award-winning author gifted at telling stories of hope and redemption. He is best known as an actor, writer, and director of the films *Fireproof, Courageous, Facing the Giants,* and *WAR ROOM* and coauthor of the New York Times bestselling books *The Love Dare, The Resolution for Men, Fireproof* (the novel), and *Courageous* (the novel). In 2002, Alex helped found Sherwood Pictures and partnered with his brother Stephen to launch Kendrick Brothers Productions. He is a graduate of Kennesaw State University and attended seminary before being ordained into ministry. Alex and his wife, Christina, live in Albany, Georgia, with their six children. They are active members of Sherwood Church.

Nic Allen serves as the Family Pastor at Rolling Hills Community Church. His undergraduate work is in Communication from Appalachian State University and he holds a Master's Degree in Christian Education from Dallas Baptist University. His passion is to disciple kids and students while equipping parents to build stronger families. Nic and his wife Susan married in 2000 and are busy raising their three kids (2 daughters; 1 son) while experiencing everything God has for them in life.

ABOUT THE MOVIE

WAR ROOM
Prayer is a Powerful Weapon

"But you, when you pray, go into your inner room, close your door and pray to your Father who is in secret, and your Father who sees what is done in secret will reward you." Matthew 6:6

From the creators of *Fireproof* and *Courageous* comes *WAR ROOM*, a compelling drama with humor and heart that explores the power prayer can have on marriages, parenting, careers, friendships, and every other area of life.

Tony and Elizabeth Jordan seemingly have it all—great jobs, a beautiful daughter, and their dream house. But appearances can be deceiving. In reality, their world is crumbling under the strain of a failing marriage. While Tony basks in his professional success, Elizabeth resigns herself to increasing bitterness. But their lives take an unexpected turn when Elizabeth meets her newest client, Miss Clara, and is challenged to establish a "war room" and a battle plan of prayer for her family. As Elizabeth tries to fight for her family, Tony's hidden struggles come to light. Tony must decide if he will make amends to his family and prove Miss Clara's wisdom that victories don't come by accident.

The movie cast features director Alex Kendrick, Priscilla Shirer, T.C. Stallings, Beth Moore, and Michael Jr., along with Karen Abercrombie as the unforgettable Miss Clara. *WAR ROOM* will inspire moviegoers to start fighting their own battles the right way—through prayer.

WWW.WARROOMTHEMOVIE.COM

FROM THE CREATORS OF FIREPROOF AND COURAGEOUS

WAR✝ROOM

PRAYER IS A POWERFUL WEAPON

INTRODUCTION

PRAYER IS A POWERFUL WEAPON

When we come to know Jesus as our Savior and Lord, our journey is only beginning. It can be easy to become wrapped up in our hectic lives and forget our first Love and the subtle Enemy who wants to keep us from Him.

In the movie *WAR ROOM*, Tony and Elizabeth Jordan are typical churchgoers who have become complacent and, in Tony's case, even hostile, toward the God who created them for His glory. The Devil is subtly wrecking their lives and marriage using their own pride, busyness, financial issues, and outside temptations.

Like the Jordans, we too can forget that our circumstances or other people are not our enemies. We can also forget about the grace and love of God and about the weapons He has given us to defeat temptation. This Bible study serves as a challenging reminder of vital truths we can easily overlook or forget.

Through this Bible study, believers will be called to evaluate their spiritual life and growth, to uncover their true character, to trust in the God of grace, to declare victory over their true Enemy, and to find their identity in their Savior. This study will serve as a reminder that prayer really is a powerful weapon.

HOW TO USE THIS STUDY

The WAR ROOM Bible Study contains five lessons that can be used for group or personal Bible study. Each lesson contains four elements: Introduction, Movie Clip Discussion, Engage Lesson, and then Devotional Homework consisting of three days of personal study. Allow 45 to 60 minutes for the group sessions.

1. INTRODUCTION: Each study begins with an introductory overview of the lesson to come. This section is designed for use in a group setting, but can also be adapted for personal study. Read through the section and answer the introductory questions together if you are in a group.

2. MOVIE CLIP DISCUSSION: The Bible study DVD contains clips from the film *WAR ROOM* to accompany each session. Each clip is 2-4 minutes in length and is supported by clip discussion questions based on the truths illustrated.

3. ENGAGE LESSON: This section is the primary focus of each week. Leaders should spend the majority of the group time teaching while using verses and questions in this section.

4. DEVOTIONAL HOMEWORK: Lastly, class members should be assigned the three days of personal Bible study with life application to complete at home during the week before the next group session. Through this personal study, members of your group will be able to dive deeper into the concepts introduced through the movie clips and group discussion.

A LETTER TO LEADERS

Thank you for answering the call to lead this small-group Bible study. Know that as we prepared this study, we have already lifted you up in prayer asking God to guide and use each leader.

We believe this study has implications for all believers. We hope it provides an opportunity for your group to grow closer to one another and ultimately, to grow closer to God as you learn together how to wield prayer as a powerful weapon.

Perhaps you are doing this study as part of a larger church-wide campaign anticipating the release of *WAR ROOM*. Perhaps your group has already seen the movie and is engaging this five-week study as a follow-up. Regardless of the timing of your study or the format of your class, this study has enormous potential to help reshape lives in your church and community as they learn more about prayer.

The words on these pages are not powerful nor are they part of a secret formula guaranteed to improve relationships and to grow your church. But combined with the life-changing, living Word of God, this message can be an incredible tool that inspires dramatic revival in the hearts of believers and offers a solid gospel tool for nonbelievers.

You may be experiencing some fear about leading this study. Don't worry! You have not been called by God to facilitate this study because you are perfect and have your life all figured out. You are leading this study because God equips His people to do His work. Our prayer for you is that as you guide this study you'll see God working in your life in mighty ways and sense the Holy Spirit carrying you.

The best way for you to prepare each week is to complete the study yourself. Be open and transparent with your group, honestly revealing areas in which you also struggle. Pray that God will direct your conversation and empower you to lead well, and He will! Thank you for leading others in this way.

For additional leader helps, visit *www.warroommovieresources.com*.

HONEST EVALUATION

This week is about evaluation. Tough questions. Real answers. This process isn't intended to make you feel ashamed, but instead to reveal blind spots and to inspire growth.

TEST YOURSELVES TO SEE IF YOU ARE IN THE FAITH. EXAMINE YOURSELVES. OR DO YOU YOURSELVES NOT RECOGNIZE THAT JESUS CHRIST IS IN YOU? —UNLESS YOU FAIL THE TEST. (2 COR. 13:5)

Welcome to week one. God created each of us for His glory and wants us to grow closer to Him and be more like Him each day. One of the most important things we can do to grow spiritually is to be truthful and open about where we are in each season. This week is about encouraging honest self-evaluation between you and God. This process isn't intended to discourage, but to help you understand yourself better and inspire you on to greater personal growth in the weeks to come.

> *In your opinion, how close are you to God right now, with zero being you are freezing cold and far away, and ten being you are on fire and extremely close?*
> 0   1   2   3   4   5   6   7   8   9   10
>
> *Regarding closeness to God, where do you want to be one year from now?*
> 0   1   2   3   4   5   6   7   8   9   10
>
> *Are you currently moving at a pace to meet your goal one year from now?*
>
> *What major decisions /adjustments do you need to make to help you grow?*

Pray now that God will give you a renewed hunger and the grace to help you to seek Him more passionately and to grow spiritually this next year. Ask Him to use this Bible study as a springboard to a deeper and closer walk with Him.

It can be very hard for us to evaluate ourselves accurately. When quizzed by others, it is human nature for us to highlight and exaggerate the good and minimize or deny what's lacking (see Prov. 21:2; 30:12; 20:6). The Apostle Paul was a prideful, self-righteous Pharisee, but after He was confronted with Jesus and the glory of God, he later called himself the chief of sinners (see 1 Tim. 1:15) Many times our actions are a much better indication of where we are spiritually than our guesses and opinions.

> *Ask yourself honestly these questions:*
>
> *1. How diligently do you seek and pursue a closer walk with God each day?*
>
> *2. How much time and effort do you spend in His Word and in prayer each week?*
>
> *3. Do you make an effort to remember and apply the Word of God after you hear it or do you usually walk away and forget it?*
>
> *4. How quickly do you obey God when He tells you to do something?*
>
> *5. When God reveals sin in your life, how quickly do you confess and repent of it?*

If you knew that Jesus was coming back in three days, what sins would you confess and quickly get out of your life? What commands would you obey between now and then? Pray now for God to give you the grace to go ahead and do these things rather than putting them off any longer.

BUT BE DOERS OF THE WORD AND NOT HEARERS ONLY, DECEIVING YOURSELVES. (JAS. 1:22)

 **MOVIE CLIP**

As a group, take time to view the "Lukewarm Coffee" clip (4:00). Read the summary statement below before watching the clip. Then take a few moments to discuss the clip using the questions provided.

SUMMARY

Elizabeth Jordan is a successful realtor living in an unsuccessful marriage. She assumes she is doing fine spiritually, but gets unexpectedly tested. A providential encounter with a new client leads to a mentoring relationship that will forever change her life. In this scene, Miss Clara asks heart-to-heart questions to help Elizabeth be open and honest about where she is spiritually.

OPEN DISCUSSION

1. *What biblical metaphor did Miss Clara use to help Elizabeth evaluate God's place in her life?*

2. *Answer the same question Miss Clara posed to Elizabeth. What is one thing about your life right now that you desire to be better? If you feel comfortable doing so, share with your group. Have you been praying about this one thing?*

3. *Do you ever feel like you are fighting the wrong fight? Explain.*

4. *What land mines are present in your life? Are there some you have stepped on? Are there some, by God's grace, you have avoided? Are there some you fear looming on the landscape of your life ahead?*

ENGAGE

Read the Scripture passage from which Miss Clara takes her lukewarm coffee analogy.

READ REVELATION 3:14-22 OUT LOUD.

Summarize Jesus' main concern with the Laodicean believers.

The Laodicean church was one marked by self-sufficiency and pride. Their city lacked a direct water supply, so aqueducts carried in hot and cold water from distant sources. But when it arrived, the water was often lukewarm and contained harmful sediments. Hot water was useful for cleaning and bathing. Cold water was useful for drinking and cooling. Lukewarm water was worthy of little more than a complaint.

How do our lives slowly become lukewarm the further we get from the Source of living water?

What evidences of lukewarm living do you see in believers' lives today? How about in your own life?

According to verse 19, what was motivating Jesus to offer such a harsh rebuke and such stern discipline? (See also Hebrews 12:6.)

What are the two things Jesus said we should do in verse 19?

Therefore be _____ and _____.

The word *zealous* means: to be filled with zeal and affection and love for someone or something. It means to get hot for God again! The word here for *repent* goes beyond merely feeling bad and regretting, but actually changing our minds and hearts about something resulting in a change of lifestyle. This is hard to do on our own, but can happen with God's help as we rely on Him.

Jesus invites us into closer and more intimate fellowship with Him. Read verse 20 again. The image of Christ standing outside the door is a message for believers who have allowed sin, apathy, and pride over time to keep Christ from His rightful throne as Lord in their lives. Jesus desires to come in closer, take rightful control, and rekindle His relationship with each of us.

What are 3 specific things in your life keeping you from being more on fire for God?
1.
2.
3.

We invite you now to pray that God will do these 3 things in your life. Ask Him to. . .
1.   Search your heart and reveal your true condition before Him.
2.   Give you the grace to repent of any unconfessed sin and be more zealous and passionate in your relationship with Him.
3.   Help you open your heart and stay obedient and intimately close to Jesus.

DAY ONE

"YOU SAY YOU ATTEND CHURCH OCCASIONALLY.
IS THAT BECAUSE YOUR PASTOR ONLY PREACHES
OCCASIONALLY?"

~MISS CLARA, WAR ROOM

This week is about spiritual evaluation. The word *evaluation* in 2 Corinthians 13:5 is taken from the Greek word *dokimazo*. It means, *to test* or *to prove*, to determine "whether a thing is genuine."[1]

There is a big difference between claiming to be a Christian and actually knowing Christ and living as a maturing believer. Anyone can claim to know Him, but those that do will experience a genuine heart transformation from the inside out (see 2 Cor. 5:17). The book of 1 John shows us that truly knowing Christ will result in a lifestyle of obedience, repentance of sin, a living faith, evidence of God's Spirit, and a love for other Christians. One such characteristic of early Christians was their willing connection to a body of believers. They wanted to share their lives with other Christians.

READ ACTS 2:44-46.

Describe the nature of the early believer's connection to one another in this passage.

Which of these experiences of the early church is most evident in the believers you know? Which do you think is most lacking? Why?

Now read 1 Corinthians 12:24b-27 below. Underline each use of the word member.

GOD HAS PUT THE BODY TOGETHER, GIVING GREATER HONOR TO
THE LESS HONORABLE, SO THAT THERE WOULD BE NO DIVISION
IN THE BODY, BUT THAT THE MEMBERS WOULD HAVE THE SAME
CONCERN FOR EACH OTHER. SO IF ONE MEMBER SUFFERS, ALL THE
MEMBERS SUFFER WITH IT; IF ONE MEMBER IS HONORED, ALL THE
MEMBERS REJOICE WITH IT. NOW YOU ARE THE BODY OF CHRIST,
AND INDIVIDUAL MEMBERS OF IT.

Describe a time of distress when you have experienced sympathy and concern from your local body of believers. You may also choose a time when you have been able to offer that same concern for someone else connected to you in the body of Christ.

Now reflect on a moment when you shared personal joy or celebration with your local body of Christ. How did your church family multiply your joy?

CLOSE TODAY'S STUDY BY READING HEBREWS 10:23-25.

For what reason(s) does the writer encourage believers to maintain faithful gatherings?

Though God is perfect, His followers on earth are not. All churches are made up of people like you and me who daily need God's grace and forgiveness. Though we each can stumble (see Jas. 3:2), God still commands all His children to stay connected—to love, serve, forgive, encourage, comfort, and pray for one another on a consistent basis. We all mutually benefit and God is glorified. It's beautiful!

Before moving on to the second session of individual study for this week, take a moment to prayerfully evaluate your connection to the local church.

If your commitment to the local church is an indication of your faith in Christ, what does it say about you?

Outside of action movies, smart soldiers don't go into battle alone. You need the local body of Christ and the local body of Christ needs you.

In closing, prayerfully ask God how He wants you to be more deeply connected to His church.

1. Thayer and Smith. "Greek Lexicon entry for Dokimazo," *The NAS New Testament Greek Lexicon* [online] 1999 (cited 2 March 2015). Available from the Internet: *www.biblestudytools.com.*

DAY TWO

"So if I asked you what your prayer life was like, would you say that it was hot or cold?"
~Miss Clara, War Room

Start today by answering Miss Clara's question. In fact, be as specific as possible using the plot line below. What is your prayer life like? Hot, cold, or somewhere in between?

COLD ●————————————————————● HOT

Perhaps the most common understanding of prayer in the life of a believer is communication with God. We talk and He listens. He speaks and we heed. At least that is how it should work, right? Many times that communication is reduced to nothing more than a list of requests begged of our benevolent God. How much would your life change if you began to view and treat God like your closest, most intimate friend rather than a casual acquaintance? What if you saw prayer as a constant necessity rather than an occasional afterthought? What if it became a ready weapon rather than a random want ad?

READ EPHESIANS 6:10-18.

How much of the armor do we daily need to put on?

In the space provided, list each part of God's armor and the purpose it wields in the life of the believer.

ARMOR	PURPOSE

Look back at Ephesians 6:11. Why is the armor so important for the believer?

The word *tactics* in the HCSB is translated as *schemes* in the NASB. In Greek, that word is *methodeia*, which means "cunning arts, deceit, crafts, and trickery." It's found only twice in the New Testament, both in Paul's letter to believers in Ephesus. The first occurrence in Ephesians 4:14 references the trickery of men. But in Ephesians 6:11, it describes the scheming lies of the Devil. Paul's recommended defense? The armor of God. One does not commonly equate prayer with battle attire, but it is no accident that Paul commands believers to pray when engaging in spiritual warfare.

Name three things we are told to do as we put on the armor of God (vs. 13,18).

According to verse 18:
When should we pray?

Whom should we pray for?

How should we pray?

Write what each phrase in verse 18 means to you:
At all times:

Every prayer and request:

Stay alert:

All perseverance:

Intercession for all the saints:

How much we pray reveals how much we depend on God. Praying is the antithesis of the self-sufficiency modeled by the Laodicean believers. Approaching God through Jesus in prayer at any time for any thing is always a priceless privilege. We all need God all the time. We need His grace moment by moment to help us not waste opportunities, not become self-centered, and not fall into sin. A richer, more active prayer life results when we humbly admit our need for Him and then daily depend on God for the wisdom and grace to do His will in each situation.

What causes you to forget your need for Christ and the armor of God?

Prayer is one of our best resources when it comes to spiritual growth. It's a weapon we have for battle. It's also the best position to be in when making evaluations. As you close today, choose a posture of submission. On your knees or lying face down, confess your great need for God. Ask Him to identify for you things you try to place before Him. Express your desire to remove those things and depend solely on Him.

Before moving on, compose a statement indicating your desire for a richer prayer life. Express to God where you would like your prayer life to go in the days ahead. Ask Him to help you get there.

DAY THREE

"YOU DON'T HAVE TO STEP ON THE SAME LAND
MINES THAT I DID. THAT'S A WASTE OF TIME."

~ MISS CLARA, WAR ROOM

In your first individual study this week, the importance of connecting deeply with a local body of believers was examined in Scripture. One of the greatest benefits to such a connection is the depth of learning that comes from walking through life with other believers. We don't have to repeat one another's mistakes. Paul wrote to Corinthian believers, "Imitate me, as I also imitate Christ" (1 Cor. 11:1). Modeling life after other seasoned believers who are slightly further along in the journey is one of the Bible's prescribed methods of discipleship.

READ HEBREWS 13:7.

CONSIDER THE FOLLOWING QUESTIONS RELATED TO THAT VERSE:

Who in your life models Christlikeness for you? What have you learned from this person?

What land mines have you avoided because of this person's wise example or counsel?

USE THE FOLLOWING QUESTIONS AS AN EVALUATION TOOL AND COMMIT TO TAKE STEPS TO IMPROVE IN THE AREAS WHERE YOU ARE LACKING:

Is your spiritual life apathetic, joyless, and passionless?

Do you have at least one sin you refuse to repent of?

Do you have at least one person you refuse to forgive?

Do you love and seek God less than you once did?

Are the words of your mouth displeasing to God and dishonorable to others?

Do you see no evidence of answered prayer or the power of God at work in your life?

Do you have time for entertainment, but not for Bible study, prayer, or sharing your faith?

Do you let pride, worry, or fear stop you from obeying what God has told you to do?

Does your family see you behave one way at church and another at home?

Is your worship of God half-hearted and mediocre?

CONCLUDE BY READING ALOUD PSALM 145:4 PROVIDED BELOW.
ONE GENERATION WILL DECLARE YOUR WORKS TO THE NEXT AND WILL PROCLAIM YOUR MIGHTY ACTS.

As a maturing believer, you are likely younger than some veteran followers of Jesus and older still than others. It is valuable to think about those whom you follow and also who follows you. How important it is for us to consider the generation coming after us and the things we may pass on of our faith, as well as the faith legacy that has been passed down to us. Reference again Paul's words in 1 Corinthians 11:1. He makes a similar statement in 1 Corinthians 4:16. Twice in this letter, he invites believers in Corinth to follow/imitate/shadow his life. Why? Because of the example of Christ he intended to set.

In the next group session, you will see a humorous clip dealing with friendship and Christian accountability—a key feature of healthy relationships. Accountability is a valuable asset in both sides of the mentoring equation. You need members of Christ's body whom you are accountable to and also those who are accountable to you. As iron sharpens iron, one friend will sharpen another (see Prov. 27:17).

Pray now for your present or future mentors and also those who will be under your care. List the names of the people in your life to whom you feel a personal responsibility to model a Christ-like example.

SESSION 2

REAL
ACCOUNTABILITY

This week is about accountability ... wounds from a trusted friend. Perhaps you have someone in your life who is willing to walk through difficulty with you. Maybe your life lacks that type of solid friendship. To have a friend like that, you should be a friend like that.

THE WOUNDS OF A FRIEND ARE TRUSTWORTHY, BUT THE KISSES OF AN ENEMY ARE EXCESSIVE. (PROV. 27:6)

Welcome to week two. Begin this week by sharing portions of your individual study experience from week one. Use the following questions as your cue:

> *What stood out most to you during last week's group discussion or devotional studies?*

> *What spiritual evaluations or commitments did God lead you to make this past week?*

AS A GROUP, READ THE FOLLOWING PSALM ALOUD. IS THIS A PRAYER YOU WOULD WILLINGLY PRAY?

Psalm 141:3-5a

LORD, SET UP A GUARD FOR MY MOUTH;
KEEP WATCH AT THE DOOR OF MY LIPS.
DO NOT LET MY HEART TURN TO ANY EVIL THING
OR PERFORM WICKED ACTS
WITH MEN WHO COMMIT SIN.
DO NOT LET ME FEAST ON THEIR DELICACIES.
LET THE RIGHTEOUS ONE STRIKE ME—
IT IS AN ACT OF FAITHFUL LOVE;
LET HIM REBUKE ME—
IT IS OIL FOR MY HEAD;
LET ME NOT REFUSE IT.

> *One of the priceless benefits of Christian community is accountability. Take time as a group to define the term. What does it look like? How is it best utilized? How have you seen it be abused?*

Proverbs 27:5-6 says, "Better is open rebuke, than love that is concealed. Faithful are the wounds of a friend, but deceitful are the kisses of an enemy" (NASB).

This week's video clip paints a clear picture of Christian accountability in action.

Comforting disclaimer: The topic of accountability can be alarming to some in a group setting. Don't worry. No one will be put on the spot. This study takes the work of spiritual evaluation you did on your own last week and establishes guardrails to keep you on track for the new commitment(s) you made.

WATCH

MOVIE CLIP

As a group, take time to view the "Weight Room" clip (2:37). Read the summary statement below before watching the clip. Then take a few moments to discuss the clip using the questions provided.

SUMMARY

Tony Jordan is far from God and making decisions some might equate with playing with fire. Fortunately for him, he has a friend willing to speak difficult truth, even when it's ill received. Michael is a genuine friend who understands much about the role of accountability. This scene depicts the importance of that value in the context of godly relationships.

OPEN DISCUSSION

1. *Explain a moment when you have been in Michael's sneakers. How was it easy or difficult for you to speak challenging words to someone you care about?*

2. *Consider a moment when you have found yourself in Tony's place. Did you have someone in your life that stepped up and confronted your sin? If so, how did you receive it?*

3. *How important is accountability in the context of Christian relationships? Why do you think that?*

ENGAGE

READ PROVERBS 27:6 AGAIN OUT LOUD (PAGE 21).

What does this passage communicate about the idea of accountability?
How is it that wounds, strikes, and rebukes from a friend can be better than kisses?

In Psalm 141, David writes favorably about accountability. His desire is for God to steer his heart away from evil, specifically by means of righteous friends who will be bold enough to rebuke a king.

As a group, read the following verses and discuss what each says about accountability.

Hebrews 3:13

Proverbs 27:17

James 5:19-20

Galatians 6:1-2

Ecclesiastes 4:9-12

In your opinion, which one of the above verses best describes the value of Christian accountability in your life?

Read Ephesians 4:15. What does it mean to "speak truth in love"? How have you seen that in action?

Do you struggle more with speaking truth or speaking in love? What are some ways someone might balance both truth and love in their communication? How did Jesus balance both?

Begin the process today as a group by reading the following prayer out loud.

Heavenly Father, you are so worthy of all our attention and affection. Each of us depends on the power of Your Holy Spirit speaking to us. Each of us needs connection to other believers who will speak hard truth in love. Will You help us balance truth and love in our relationships? Will You help us practice true Christian accountability? We love You. We believe that You hear us and know our heart's desire to follow You well. In unity of heart and spirit we pray in Jesus' name. Amen.

DAY ONE

In your individual study this week, you will continue to press in to the value of accountability within your Christian community. While the Bible doesn't offer us a simple recipe for accountability with other believers, ingredients can be found throughout the Old and New Testaments.

READ EPHESIANS 5:1-14.

Take a moment to be vulnerable. Although this portion of your *WAR ROOM* study centers on the need for accountability with other believers, this time is just between you and God.

> *What in your past or present resembles a fruitless "work of darkness" described by Paul in Ephesians 5:11? In an attitude of confession, compose a list below of things you need to get out of your life.*

> *Read 1 John 1:8-9 and note specifically what it states as a benefit of confession before God.*

Now be honest. Is there another trusted believer who could have also composed your list? Someone who knows where your weaknesses and blind spots really are?

NOW READ JAMES 5:16.

> *What benefit is there to sharing struggles with another believer?*

The Greek word for *healing* in this verse is *iaomai*. Of course, it means exactly what you think it means … *cured*. But there is a secondary meaning that might communicate more accurately what confession does. It means *to be made whole*.[1] That is certainly what happens at the moment of salvation. It's also what can happen in our hearts when we walk in accountable connection to other believers. Wholeness. Healing.

Have you experienced or witnessed the healing power of an accountability relationship with another believer? If yes, describe it below.

It's in darkness that someone screams, "none of your business." Ultimately, we were made for connections. The best picture of Christianity is when we walk in healthy and honest relationships so that others can see Christ by our love for one another.

Read Isaiah 29:15 and copy the prophet's words in the space below.

Confessing brings forgiveness and healing.

Concealing brings grief and pain.

Compare and contrast Ephesians 5:11-12 and Psalm 66:18.

How has unconfessed sin affected your prayer life?

Do you have someone who holds you accountable for sinful patterns in your life? Think about who you might approach to begin an accountability relationship. Make plans to talk with them about beginning this sort of relationship.

Secret sins lead to shame and unheard prayers. In closing, pray to the God who hears you because He has forgiven you. Thank Him for that. Then ask Him to bring accountability to walk in healing, wholeness, and the confidence that your prayers are heard.

1. Thayer and Smith. "Greek Lexicon entry for Iaomai," *The NAS New Testament Greek Lexicon* [online] 1999 (cited 2 March 2015). Available from the Internet: *www.biblestudytools.com*.

DAY TWO

"SINCE WE'VE BEEN FRIENDS FOR A LONG TIME, I'M
NOT JUST GONNA WATCH YOUR MARRIAGE DIE. SO
IF IT'S BLEEDING, I'M NOT JUST GONNA KEEP EATING
MY SALAD."

~ MICHAEL, WAR ROOM

There is a great responsibility in relationships. Look up and read each of the following verses. Note the aspect of responsibility present in each passage.

Ephesians 4:29-32

John 15:13

Job 6:14

Proverbs 18:24

Part of having a Christian community is having friends who will walk through difficulty with you and also hold you accountable to your commitment to Christ. We are never so vulnerable to sin than when we are alone. We need community to remind us to remain strong.

ONE WHO ISOLATES HIMSELF PURSUES SELFISH DESIRES; HE REBELS
AGAINST ALL SOUND JUDGMENT. (PROV. 18:1)

A good accountability partner can be trusted to keep a confidence. Closeness in relationships is built upon trust (see Prov. 11:13).

READ 1 CORINTHIANS 12:12-26.

These verses talk about the diversity of gifts and talents among the body of believers. Instead of holding one person or one talent above the others, we are to work together to help one another grow toward Christlikeness.

Think about the diversity of gifts and talents in your church and in your small group. List some of the gifts members of your community have that you do not possess.

In what ways have you seen your community use their gifts and talents to help someone when they were "bleeding"?

In what ways have you worked together to spur one another toward Christlikeness?

This passage also talks about having the "same concern for each other" (v. 25). Paul goes on to say this means we are to suffer with those in our community who suffer. We are also to rejoice when those in our community are honored. This is often much easier said than done.

How have you seen the church suffer with one another? How have you seen them rejoice with one another?

What are some steps you can take as a group to better use your talents and abilities to suffer and to rejoice with one another?

How can you take steps personally to suffer and rejoice with your community of believers?

Without one another, the body of believers would be incomplete. God has given us each other so that we may grow to be more like Him. We do that best in community and accountability with one another.

As you close this session of individual study, compose a prayer, praying specifically for each of the items below:

- *Offer praise to God for Jesus Christ, the Messiah.*
- *Thank God for your network of brothers and sisters in Christ.*
- *Ask Him to strengthen your church family.*
- *If you have a specific brother or sister in Christ you would name as an accountability partner, thank God for that person.*
- *If you do not have an accountability partner, ask God to send you one.*
- *Ask God to strengthen your ability to speak truth in love to friends who depend on you for accountability.*
- *Ask God to continue to reveal areas of weakness in your life that need a greater focus on Him.*
- *Thank Him for hearing and providing.*

DAY THREE

What do you suppose it means to "see the church" in someone? Perhaps the question can be made clearer this way: What does it mean to live in a way that reflects Christ, as His church? Journal your response below.

The Bible doesn't use the word "accountability" directly, but it repeatedly describes accountable relationships using other biblical virtues and admonitions.

I AM THE LORD YOUR GOD, WHO BROUGHT YOU OUT OF THE
LAND OF EGYPT SO THAT YOU WOULD NOT BE THEIR SLAVES, AND
I BROKE THE BARS OF YOUR YOKE AND MADE YOU WALK ERECT.
(LEV. 26:13, NASB)

The word *erect* is the Hebrew word *komemeeyooth* and is written as *freely* or *freedom* in other biblical translations. Uprightness is another word for integrity.[1] While sin can enslave us (see John 8:34), helping each other to avoid sin actually brings greater freedom. Being in accountable relationships with other believers helps us not only to walk in integrity, but to avoid the consequences of foolish decisions while enjoying the benefits and of doing the right thing.

THE HIGHWAY OF THE UPRIGHT IS TO DEPART FROM EVIL;

HE WHO WATCHES HIS WAY PRESERVES HIS LIFE. (PROV. 16:17)

Being accountable to God because of the great gift of freedom He has afforded us in Christ prompts us toward obedience. Our accountability to one another is a reflection of that freedom lived responsibly.

Look up the verses below. Beside each, note what they say explicitly about freedom. Then write what is implied about responsibility.

Psalm 119:45

2 Corinthians 3:17

Galatians 5:1

Romans 6:22

The root mark of a believer in Jesus Christ is freedom. The greatest joy of any church, the collective body of Christ, should be the freedom that we have from the consequences of sin.

Walking in freedom from sin doesn't indicate freedom from responsibility. In fact, our freedom in Christ creates responsibility for our actions. Fortunately for us, we have the power of the Holy Spirit working in our lives transforming us into living, breathing images of Jesus.

Even if someone is not in our accountability group, both in Matthew 18:15-18 and Luke 17:3, Jesus communicates that we should go to other believers privately when needed and hold them accountable when they are living in sin. While this is never fun, it is a necessary part of us helping each other stay right with the Lord.

> *Finally, close in prayer continuing to ask God to strengthen existing relationships or to birth new ones for the purpose of holding you accountable to His Word. The goal? So that others may see the beauty and integrity of Christ and the glory of God in you and your church.*

1. Brown, Driver, Briggs, and Gesenius.. "Hebrew Lexicon entry for Qowmemiyuwth," *The NAS Old Testament Hebrew Lexicon* [online] (cited 2 March 2015). Available from the Internet: www. biblestudytools.com.

SESSION 3

LIVING THE GOSPEL

This week is about gospel power. The gospel doesn't just save us from hell. Christ's kingdom is one where the inhabitants' lives are transformed daily to look more like Him. Scripture calls this sanctification. So it's not only by God's grace that we are saved. It is by God's grace that we are changed.

AND GOD IS ABLE TO MAKE EVERY GRACE OVERFLOW TO YOU, SO THAT IN EVERY WAY, ALWAYS HAVING EVERYTHING YOU NEED, YOU MAY EXCEL IN EVERY GOOD WORK. (2 COR. 9:8)

Definitions matter. Today we challenge you to come up with a definition of grace.

READ EPHESIANS 2:4-9.

The word *grace* is used three times in this passage. The entire passage ties grace and salvation to love, kindness, riches, and God freely meeting significant spiritual needs in our lives that we did not earn or deserve. Using Ephesians 2:4-9, take a moment to quickly craft your own group definition of grace. Let each participant share and then whittle each idea into a single, agreed upon, definition. Record your definition.

> *Group definition of grace:*

Discuss the following to begin your group study today.

> *Why is it so important to understand God's grace as an unmerited gift of His favor and kindness?*

> *Why is a works-based understanding of salvation wrong?*

> *Why would human pride tend to choose a works-based salvation?*

> *How is a works-based salvation actually oppressive, enslaving, and discouraging?*

Salvation by grace through faith separates Christianity from ever other religion in the world. However, our understanding of grace should not be limited to the atonement offered us by Christ's death. It should also extend to the change and new life wrought in us by His resurrection and through the giving of the Holy Spirit that follows one's salvation. Even as we relied on God's grace to be saved, we must also rely on His grace daily to freely provide us with everything we need to obey Him and live out His commands.

Now, how does understanding and receiving God's grace cause us to treat others differently? How might God's gifts of kindness to us make us into more giving and kind people? How does being forgiven by grace enable us to freely forgive others?

WATCH

As a group, take time to view the "Gospel and Grace" clip (3:51). Read the summary statement below before watching the clip. Then take a few moments to discuss the clip using the questions provided.

SUMMARY

Elizabeth is now growing in a mentoring relationship with Miss Clara. In this clip from the movie *WAR ROOM,* Miss Clara seizes a teachable moment to guide Elizabeth in her understanding of grace. Miss Clara invites Elizabeth to better understand the grace given to her by God. She also alerts Elizabeth to the attacks of her Enemy who wants nothing more than to destroy Elizabeth's understanding and utilization of God's grace.

OPEN DISCUSSION

1. *Who has extended great grace to you in the past? Or who has taught you a great deal about how to walk in grace? What have you learned from them?*

2. *Have you had difficulty in your life forgiving those who have wronged you? If yes, why do you think that is true?*

3. *How does Miss Clara describe the gospel in this clip?*

4. *According to Miss Clara, what do we deserve from God? How do you respond knowing He offers grace instead?*

5. *How aware are you of the real Enemy's attacks in your life?*

ENGAGE

Using the Ephesians 2:4-9 passage read earlier, answer the questions below.

What do these verses say about the character and heart of our God?

According to this passages, why has God granted us grace and forgiveness?

What danger is associated with works in Ephesians 2:9?

Works-based salvation is actually impossible and seeks to honor man. Grace-based salvation is what Jesus offers us and honors God alone. Now read the following passages about living in God's grace. Using the questions provided, discuss what these passages offer regarding sanctification (becoming more like Christ).

Colossians 3:12-17
Titus 2:11-14
Ephesians 4:22-32

Based on these passages, in light of the salvation we have been given, how are believers to live? How are they not to live?

According to Colossians 3:13, we are to forgive as we have been forgiven. Why is that such an important part of grace?

Taking off the old self and putting on the new self is a vivid description of what happens in the life of a believer walking in God's grace. To put on a new self is to take action. We are to walk like Jesus walked. Everything about a person's life after salvation is a work in progress moving the believer ever closer to the image of Jesus.

Have you been trying to work and earn salvation by your religious deeds and performance or have you truly received by faith the free gift of forgiveness and salvation by God's grace and what Christ has already done for you? If you have been trying to earn your way into Heaven, then is anything stopping you from right now trusting Christ and His death on the cross as full payment of your sins? Pray now and receive His free gift of eternal life by faith. (See Romans 6:23.)

How might you pray for one another to experience God's grace and walk fully alive in it this week? Invite volunteers to pray, thanking God for His grace and asking for His help and strength to forgive and extend kindness to others as Christ has modeled for you.

DAY ONE

"HE GIVES US GRACE AND HE HELPS US TO GIVE IT
TO OTHERS EVEN WHEN THEY DON'T DESERVE IT. WE
ALL DESERVE JUDGMENT. AND THAT IS WHAT A HOLY
GOD GIVES US WHEN WE DON'T REPENT AND BELIEVE
IN HIS SON."

~MISS CLARA, WAR ROOM

In your individual studies this week, you will first evaluate the power of the gospel in your life. Grace is God's free gift. No one earns it. No one could. That's what makes it good news. The grace of God is not only what saves you. It also sustains you. And you never need it more than when you are faced with your Enemy.

Start today with some gospel exploration.

Read the following verses and describe what each says about grace and/or the gospel.

Romans 5:8

Romans 6:23

Romans 8:1

2 Corinthians 5:21

1 Timothy 1:15

DIVE IN TO ROMANS 3:23-26.

FOR ALL HAVE SINNED AND FALL SHORT OF THE GLORY OF
GOD. THEY ARE JUSTIFIED FREELY BY HIS GRACE THROUGH THE
REDEMPTION THAT IS IN CHRIST JESUS. GOD PRESENTED HIM
AS A PROPITIATION THROUGH FAITH IN HIS BLOOD, TO DEMON-
STRATE HIS RIGHTEOUSNESS, BECAUSE IN HIS RESTRAINT GOD
PASSED OVER THE SINS PREVIOUSLY COMMITTED. GOD PRESENTED

HIM TO DEMONSTRATE HIS RIGHTEOUSNESS AT THE PRESENT TIME, SO THAT HE WOULD BE RIGHTEOUS AND DECLARE RIGHTEOUS THE ONE WHO HAS FAITH IN JESUS.

Underline everything God has done for you in this passage.

Now write everything you have done to earn God's grace, according to this passage.

The Greek word for *fall* is *hustereo* and literally means *behind*. To fall behind means to miss the goal. It also bears the connotation to be inferior or to fail.[1]

All we bring to salvation is a life that falls completely behind. Why? Because of sin. What God does, in spite of our sin, is grant grace and righteousness in sin's place. Nothing we do could have ever come close, much less crossed the finish line of salvation. Only by God's grace can we be forgiven.

What is the appropriate response to this passage and to God's gift of grace and love for us?

Write a prayer of thanksgiving to God, thanking Him for His grace and forgiveness.

If you have not yet surrendered your life to Jesus, accepting His gift of grace to cover your sin, seek counsel from your small group leader, a pastor, or another godly friend. Consider praying the prayer below in your own words.

God, I know I am unworthy of Your grace and Your presence. Forgive me for my disobedience. Thank You for sending Your Son to cover my sinfulness on the cross. Thank You for Your gift of grace. I submit my life to You. Help me to live as a new creation. Amen.

1. Thayer and Smith. "Greek Lexicon entry for hustereo," *The NAS New Testament Greek Lexicon* [online] 1999 (cited 2 March 2015). Available from the Internet: *www.biblestudytools.com*.

DAY TWO

"Elizabeth, there's not room for you and God on the throne of your heart. It's either Him or it's you. You need to step down. If you want victory, you have to first surrender."

~MISS CLARA, WAR ROOM

START TODAY BY READING 1 SAMUEL 5:1-6.

Two things from this story are clear.

1. God had no intention of sharing space with a false idol in a temple.

2. God has no intention of sharing space in our hearts with false idols either.

At the core, salvation is a priceless gift from God. It also beautifully leads to the most unnatural action from those who have received it—surrender. Surrender is unnatural because it feels like giving up, giving in.

It's far more natural to fight for control. It's far easier to give in to our flesh and preserve our own ego and status. But it's also far more damaging.

J.D. Greear writes, "The gospel has done its work in us when we crave God more than we crave everything else in life—more than money, romance, family, health, fame—and when seeing His kingdom advance in the lives of others gives us more joy than anything we could own. When we see Jesus as greater than anything the world can offer, we'll gladly let everything else go to possess Him."[1]

What do you crave most? List anything and everything you tend to place first in your life ahead of God.

Would you be willing to lay aside these or anything else, even good things, in order to keep Christ first in your heart?

Perhaps Elizabeth was reluctant to offer Tony grace because she didn't understand the fullness of God's grace in her own life. The gospel of Jesus is cheap if those who have received it can't be distributors of it. Only when we come down off the throne of our lives can we truly see how much God has given us. Then, and only then, will we desire Him more than anything else the world offers.

READ MATTHEW 13:44-46.

Summarize the two simple illustrations found in these parables.

What was required of the man and the merchant to gain their treasures? How does that illustrate the kingdom of heaven?

If we want victory, it starts with surrender. Surrender feels unnatural until you understand that what you gain by surrendering to Christ is better than anything you could ever want in His place.

List the ways you need to surrender to God in the following areas:

In your family:

In your marriage:

At your church:

In the way you use your time and resources:

Close today by composing a prayer of surrender. Tell God how grateful you are for grace. Ask Him to help you give Him His rightful place on the throne of your life. Tell Him exactly how blessed you feel to have Him first. Express to Him your desire to keep it that way.

FOR WHOEVER WISHES TO SAVE HIS LIFE WILL LOSE IT, BUT WHOEVER LOSES HIS LIFE FOR MY SAKE AND THE GOSPEL'S WILL SAVE IT. (MARK 8:35, NASB)

1. J. D. Greear, *Gospel* (Nashville, TN: B&H Publishing, 2011), 23.

DAY THREE

"YOU NEED TO DO YOUR FIGHTING IN PRAYER."
~MISS CLARA, WAR ROOM

There is perhaps nothing more worshipful than vulnerability. Why? Two reasons. First, being vulnerable indicates trust and humility of heart. Second, being vulnerable before God indicates a truer understanding of who He is—that He is trustworthy. A high view of God in a time of need draws the believer ever closer to the only One who can meet every need.

Start today by taking time to memorize Hebrews 4:16.

> THEREFORE LET US APPROACH THE THRONE OF GRACE WITH
> BOLDNESS, SO THAT WE MAY RECEIVE MERCY AND FIND GRACE TO
> HELP US AT THE PROPER TIME.

To approach God boldly does not mean we can approach Him disrespectfully or pridefully—but as God's children enjoying a "freedom of speech" before our loving Father. Because of what Jesus has done for us we are no longer enemies inhibited by sin, guilt, shame, or doubt. We are beloved children who, by faith, can pray openly and freely with confidence in our Father's care for us and ability to handle any request.

Describe the time in your life when you felt you needed God's help the most.

God is in the business of using the weak for His purposes. One might argue it is the key God uses to unlock His power. Take a look at these examples and note how God uses the weak in mighty ways:

1. Peter's weakness—John 18:25-27

   How God used Peter—Acts 2:37:42

2. Moses' weakness—Exodus 3:1-10; 4:10-13

   How God used Moses—Exodus 13:1-16

3. Gideon's weakness—Judges 6:11-16

   How God used Gideon—Judges 8:22-35

Gideon's legacy wasn't what you might expect. Why?

How has God used weakness in your life to show His power?

How likely are you to seek God's help first when encountering a problem (before exhausting other resources)? Mark your response on the line provided.

NOT VERY
LIKELY

EXTREMELY
LIKELY

READ 1 CORINTHIANS 1:26-31.

Fill in the blanks based on the passage.

GOD CHOOSES THE _____ TO SHAME THE

_____ AND THE _____ TO

SHAME THE _____. (V. 27)

SO THAT _____. (V. 29)

Take time to confess to God some key areas in your life where you have been trying to use your own strength.

Pray now that God will be made strong in all your weaknesses. Ask Him to remove anything that would hinder you from praying freely, confidently, and boldly. Ask Him to deepen your trust and faith in His love and ability to handle any request.

Now close by lifting up a specific need or concern before His throne that you or your family have right now. Tell Him that you are trusting Him to intervene and do what is best in this situation. Ask Him to give you a story you can share with others that will honor Him regarding how He answers.

SESSION 4

VICTORY ACCOMPLISHED

Who is the Enemy? Is it a red-horned, pitchfork-wielding cartoon character with a wicked smile? Hardly. There is a dangerous Enemy bent on destroying you. This week is about claiming truth, leaning in toward the power of the gospel, and walking in the victory that has already been accomplished in Christ.

YOU ARE FROM GOD, LITTLE CHILDREN, AND YOU HAVE CONQUERED THEM, BECAUSE THE ONE WHO IS IN YOU IS GREATER THAN THE ONE WHO IS IN THE WORLD. (1 JOHN 4:4)

Welcome to week four. Begin this week by sharing portions of your individual study experience together. Use the following questions as cues.

What stood out most to you during last week's personal Bible study?

How did God speak or guide you this week? How did you see His grace at work?

As a believer's understanding of grace expands, he or she starts to see God's grace as not only what saves us but also what sustains us. In the difficulties of life, Christians need to see evidence of that life-giving grace. When it comes to dealing with the attacks of our Enemy, we need that grace more than ever.

When it comes to Satan, people have varying beliefs regarding his existence or activity in their lives. There are those who completely deny the presence of the devil and others who not only believe in him, but blame him for every traffic light and rainy day. Some are unaware and are "ignorant of his schemes" (2 Cor. 2:11) and others may tend to overemphasize his wiles and fail to absorb human responsibility or recognize divine providence. Regardless, it is important that our theology regarding the devil stay balanced and biblical.

Over a dozen books in the Bible reference the Devil and Jesus Himself testified to his existence (see Luke 10:18-20), talked to him (see Luke 4), taught about him (see John 8:42-44), and warned about him (see Luke 22:31). The Bible refers to him by many names including: Satan, the Devil, the serpent of old, the dragon, and the accuser of the brethren (see Rev. 12:7-12). Paul said, "for we are not ignorant of his schemes" (2 Cor. 2:11, NASB).

> BE OF SOBER SPIRIT, BE ON THE ALERT. YOUR ADVERSARY, THE DEVIL, PROWLS AROUND LIKE A ROARING LION, SEEKING SOMEONE TO DEVOUR. BUT RESIST HIM, FIRM IN YOUR FAITH. (1 PET. 5:8-9)

DISCUSS THE FOLLOWING BEFORE VIEWING THE MOVIE CLIP FOR THIS WEEK:

How has your understanding of Satan evolved from childhood to today?

How do you tend to deny or downplay the Devil or overemphasize his role in your life?

How have you seen the Enemy actively attempt to destroy you and/or others around you?

MOVIE CLIP

As a group, take time to view the "Kicking Out the Devil" clip (3:53). Read the summary statement below before watching the clip. Then take a few moments to discuss the clip using the questions provided.

SUMMARY

There is a distinct difference between acquiring knowledge and applying it. This clip offers a glimpse into the latter as Elizabeth takes the truth she has learned from Miss Clara home with her. In her prayer, Elizabeth transitions from pleading with God to denying the Enemy entry into her home, her life, and her family. She moves from earnestly praying Scripture to boldly resisting Satan and declaring victory over him.

OPEN DISCUSSION

1. *What was different about Elizabeth's prayer as she made her way through the den and onto the porch?*

2. *Why do you think reading or reciting Scripture is such a powerful way to pray?*

3. *Consider how you tend to regard the Enemy. Is he someone you fear or are you keenly aware of Christ's victory over him? Explain.*

The Bible communicates that the Holy Spirit in the hearts of believers is much more powerful than the Devil. The Apostle John wrote, "You are from God, little children, and have overcome them; because greater is He who is in you than he who is in the world." (1 John 4:4-5, NASB).

> *The Holy Spirit also helps us in our prayer lives. Read Romans 8:26-27 about the power of the Spirit regarding prayer. Fill in the blanks with a word birthed out of your understanding of each verse.*
>
> *Romans 8:26*   *"The Holy Spirit* _____ *for*
> *me when I do not know what to pray."*
>
> *Romans 8:27*   *"The Holy Spirit prays for us according to the*
> _____ *of God."*
>
> *What does the passage say the Holy Spirit does for us when we don't know how to pray?*

We pray for needs and issues of which we are personally and consciously aware. However the Holy Spirit is omniscient and knows what we also should be praying. He not only inspires us with additional things to ask, but He intercedes to the Father on our behalf with requests beyond our ability or comprehension. He prays for us perfectly according to the will of God with groanings "too deep for words" (NASB).

Believers need the power of the Holy Spirit present in prayer because that's where the real battle takes place. In the film, Elizabeth learns that her real enemy is not her husband. Her real enemy is Satan and the real struggle is how much footing he has in her life.

> *What does it mean to give the Devil an opportunity?*
>
> *Bitterness clearly gives the Enemy a foothold that he uses to build a stronghold. How does Ephesians 4:30-32 say we should deal with bitterness?*
>
> *What other sins might give the Devil ground to attack us and build a stronghold? (See 1 Samuel 15:23; Acts 19:18-19; 1 Corinthians 6:15-20)*
>
> *What role does prayer play in not giving the Devil an opportunity?*

To close your group study, assign each person someone to pray for in the group. Use this time to pray in the power of the Holy Spirit. Also by faith ask the Holy Spirit to intercede on your behalf and pray for you to the Father according to the will of God.

DAY ONE

"Submit to God. Resist the Devil and he will flee." [James 4:7]

~ELIZABETH, WAR ROOM

Miss Clara, the catalytic character from *WAR ROOM*, knows many things well. She knows God's Word and how to apply it. When it comes to gospel impact, you can't have one without the other. Of course Jesus summed it up best. He explained that anyone who not only hears His words but also applies them is wise (see Matt. 7:24-25).

BEGIN TODAY BY READING JOHN 10:10.

> A thief comes only to steal and to kill and to destroy. I have come so that they may have life and have it in abundance.

Satan is a thief who does come to steal from you. But it isn't petty theft. It's more akin to felony murder. But it goes deeper still. His is a premeditated assault bent on destroying our joy, faith, family, and testimony. It is important to know our Enemy and understand his attacks.

Read the following passages. Match from the adjacent list what each says about Satan and his attacks.

Revelation 12:10	A liar and the father of liars
John 8:44	Ruler of this world who uses the disobedient
1 Peter 5:8	Looks for anyone he can devour
Ephesians 2:2	Blinds unbelievers
2 Corinthians 4:4	Employs tactics to tempt
Ephesians 6:11	Accuses day and night

In John 10:10, what does John say Jesus comes to give?

Jesus comes to give life, but Satan's goal is to destroy.

Take a moment to be candid. If you need a boost of clarity, ask the Holy Spirit to reveal important truths to you. If you need a boost of courage, ask the same Spirit to endow you with strength.

For each of the following, name the method that the Enemy uses to attack you.

- *How does the Enemy distract you?*

- *How does the Enemy deceive you?*

- *How does the Enemy divide you?*

- *What does Satan work to destroy in your life?*

READ JAMES 4:7.

THEREFORE, SUBMIT TO GOD. BUT RESIST THE DEVIL, AND HE WILL FLEE FROM YOU.

It is what you need to remember first when dealing with Satan's desire to steal, kill, and destroy you. Submit to God. We talked about that last week.

How does submitting to God bring life rather than destruction?

This verse also shows the Devil can be resisted. When he is resisted, he will flee. That is a divine promise. It's evidence of God's grace. It is very good news.

Close in prayer this week praising God for that promise and declaring your own intention to resist the Enemy when he tries to distract, deceive, and divide you from the Lord and others. It starts by taking God at His word and submitting to the lordship of Christ. You do that best in a posture of prayer.

DAY TWO

"YOU HAVE PLAYED WITH MY MIND AND HAD YOUR
WAY LONG ENOUGH. NO MORE. YOU ARE DONE."
~ELIZABETH, WAR ROOM

As Elizabeth prayed in her closet, she cried out to God. In essence, she begged for help. The very next line she uttered was Scripture. When God comes to our rescue, it is often with His Word.

> *Read the following verses Elizabeth recites in her earnest prayer. Then record them in the space provided.*
>
> *John 10:10*
>
> *2 Thessalonians 3:3*
>
> *James 4:7*

Those words from the Bible provided all the ammunition Elizabeth needed to stand up and fight against the Enemy in the manner Miss Clara prescribed.

When you read the verses in the order Elizabeth recited them, it makes a great deal of sense. The first reference unveils the true nature of the Enemy's game. He comes to steal, kill, and destroy. John 10:10 also reveals to us God's promise in response to the Evil One. Jesus has come to give life, to offer back what sin takes away. Second Thessalonians 3:3 explains how that life is possible. When the Devil attacks, the Lord provides strength. It is He who guards us. Finally, James 4:7 gives the prescription for how 2 Thessalonians 3:3 works. The believer must submit to God and resist the Devil. Then, he will flee.

Understand the Enemy. (John 10:10)

Trust in God's defense. (2 Thessalonians 3:3)

Submit to God's will. (James 4:7)

That is a fairly simple plan with an often-difficult application.

Which strategy (or verse) is most difficult for you and why?

It is not an accident that Elizabeth used Scripture to gain confidence and boldly stand up to the Enemy.

READ EPHESIANS 6:17.

What does this verse say about the Word of God?

How is it that God's Word can be a weapon in your life?

Filling your mind with Scripture is the best way to ready yourself for battle. We know this because of Jesus' example.

READ MATTHEW 4:1-11.

How did Jesus respond to the Devil's questions?

Jesus used Scripture as a weapon against Satan. He not only knew Bible verses, but knew their context. He had meditated on them and studied them. He realized Scripture can be used as a weapon to defeat temptation and Satan.

READ 2 TIMOTHY 3:16-17.

List the ways Paul declares that God's Word is useful.

Scripture is inspired by God, so it is a powerful sword He Himself has given us. With His Word, we can teach, we can rebuke, we can be equipped for every good work. We also have the power to defeat Satan when we wield the weapon of the Word.

What do you need to do in order to be prepared to wield Scripture as a weapon against temptation? How can you take steps to do that this week?

Ask God for help in studying and learning His Word. Thank Him for giving us the weapon to overcome Satan and the means to be equipped for every good work. Pray that He will guide you to specific verses to learn that will help you to respond to the Enemy's lies with God's unchanging Truth.

DAY THREE

"My joy doesn't come from my friends. It doesn't come from my job. It doesn't even come from my husband. My joy is found in Jesus, and just in case you forgot, He has already defeated you."

~ELIZABETH, WAR ROOM

It's been taught that happiness is delight based on circumstances while joy is delight regardless of circumstances. While happiness can often be mistaken for joy when all in life seems right, it is only through a relationship with Christ that a person can have true joy even when everything is terribly wrong.

Take a moment to describe a time when you experienced joy during difficulty.

Now, consider the source of that joy. The easy "church" answer is: Jesus. But for this exercise, we want you to share in the space provided what specifically about Jesus brings you joy.

Read through the following principles regarding joy and the Scripture verses that accompany each.

Psalm 71:23	Joy is present in my life when I am praising God.
Psalm 21:6	I have joy when I am in God's presence.
James 1:2-3	I may have joy in trials because God gives me endurance.
Psalm 119:11	Joy comes from knowing the Word of God.
1 Peter 1:8	Joy is found through faith in Christ.
Philemon 1:7	Joy comes from encouragement and fellowship with other believers.
Galatians 5:22	Joy comes through the working of the Holy Spirit.

Paul sat in prison as he wrote Philippians, perhaps his most joyful letter. He mentions joy and rejoicing many times and in Philippians 4:4, he tells the Philippians to "rejoice always."

READ PHILIPPIANS 4:4-9.

What does it look like to "rejoice always"? When times are good? When times are difficult?

What does Paul suggest we do in order to have the "peace of God"?

Paul wrote to the Philippians that they should stop worrying and go to God with their requests. He follows by saying they were to dwell (reckon, measure, or deliberate) on things that are lovely, pure, and true. There is no one more true, lovely, excellent, and praiseworthy than God Himself. And there is no word truer, purer, lovelier, or more excellent than the very words of God. There is nothing that can give us peace and joy like prayer, fixing our eyes on Jesus, and Scripture.

In his reality-based fiction work, *The Screwtape Letters,* C.S. Lewis explores the attacks of the Enemy against the children of God. He writes in the voice of a demon, "It is funny how mortals always picture us as putting things into their minds: in reality our best work is done by keeping things out."[1]

One of the strategies the Enemy employs is to turn your thoughts away from God, away from joy. Perhaps he doesn't do that best by entering your mind but by preventing you from dwelling on that which would undoubtedly turn you toward God.

As you close today, ask God to turn your mind toward the those things listed in Philippians 4:8. Ask Him to help you dwell on Him and His Word. Turn anything you have recently been worried about into a prayer request. Cast your cares upon the Lord and then thank God for the joy found only in Him.

1. C. S. Lewis, *The Screwtape Letters,* New York, NY: Harper Collins, 1996), 16.

IMPACTED BY GRACE

This final week is about identity in Jesus. It's the culmination of the weeks of evaluation and declaration you have experienced. It's a reality forged by the power of the Holy Spirit in our lives. It's a connection point with God best illustrated through a deepening prayer life. Being forgiven of sin and impacted by grace transforms a person. This week's Bible study is an examination of what that transformation can truly be like.

BUT TO ALL WHO DID RECEIVE HIM, HE GAVE THEM THE RIGHT TO BE CHILDREN OF GOD, TO THOSE WHO BELIEVE IN HIS NAME. (JOHN 1:12)

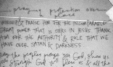

Welcome to week five. Begin this week by sharing portions of your individual study experience together. Take time for each participant who is willing to answer one or more of the following questions:

- *How did God speak directly to you this week through your personal Bible study?*

- *In what ways have you seen God's Spirit active in you this week?*

- *Who has been the most influential person in your life regarding your identity in Christ? Why?*

One of the most interesting undertakings of any faith-based film is the journey of a character. It's one thing to see where a character begins and note where they are as the movie ends. It's another to note the specific parts of the journey that take them there. Taking off an old self and putting on a new one is an active part of being a Christ follower. As we learned in week three, it's called sanctification and it's the work of the Holy Spirit shaping us into the image of Jesus. That process is worth noting in each of our lives.

As you start this week, take time to list five to seven characteristics of a transformed life.

Now make it a little more personal. What has been the most transformational experience in your life as a believer? Share with the group.

Charles Stanley explains that Christian transformation, like restoring old furniture, is a two-stage process. First, one must take off the old. Then, you have a clean slate to put on the new.[1] This week's clip offers a glimpse into that process. As you watch, consider the work that God has done in your life to help you take off the old and put on the new. As you do, remember that the process of pruning in your life is an important step towards God's desired outcome, and recognize that God is still working in your life to shape you into the person He created you to be.

1. Charles Stanley, *A Touch of His Freedom* (Grand Rapids, MI: Zondervan, 1991), 27.

MOVIE CLIP

As a group, take time to view the "Tony's Apology" clip (3:29). Read the summary statement below before watching the clip. Then take a few moments to discuss the clip using the questions provided.

SUMMARY

The movie *WAR ROOM* is full of turning points. By far, the most significant is Tony's. From self-focused to Christ-centered. From proud sinner to humble and repentant. From absentee husband to devoted believer. Grace and forgiveness can change a person. So can prayer. This scene paints a picture of repentance and forgiveness that viewers need to see. It's a picture of answered prayer resulting in life transformation.

OPEN DISCUSSION

1. *Why is it so important that Elizabeth declare to whom she truly belongs?*

2. *Tony doesn't understand the nature of Elizabeth's forgiveness. Have you ever wrestled with the idea of being forgiven? How?*

3. *How have you been changed by someone's prayers for you? How have you seen change in someone else as an answer to your own prayers?*

4. *What difference did it make in Elizabeth's life when she discovered from where her contentment must come? How did it affect her relationship with Tony?*

Read Galatians 2:19b-20. Underline the phrase, "I no longer live, but Christ lives in me."

How do you see that phrase present in Tony's life?

Based on both this week's and last week's clips, how is that phrase present in Elizabeth's life?

Think through your own story. What is something God has done in you (through sanctification) to make Galatians 2:20 true in your life? Share that with your group.

READ JESUS' WORDS TO HIS DISCIPLES IN JOHN 15:1-8.

As a group, list Christ's primary instructions for His followers.

What does Jesus say about Himself and what does He promise to do in this passage?

The word for *remain* or *abide* in this passage is the Greek word *meno*. In addition to simply remaining or abiding, it means *to continue to be present* or *to be held*, or *kept continually*. There is the idea of lasting or enduring. Jesus wants us to stay in close fellowship with Him and never pull away.

Fruit is the Greek word *karpos*. It is the outcome or result of remaining connected to Christ, the Vine. Look up the following verses and discuss the types of fruit God seeks.

Galatians 5:22
Hebrews 13:15
Romans 6:22
Colossians 1:10
Romans 10:13-15

How are you intentionally staying connected to the Vine? What fruit is present in your life as a result of remaining close to Christ?

USE THE FOLLOWING PRAYER AS A PROMPT TO CLOSE THIS FINAL GROUP TIME.

Heavenly Father, we cannot be more like Christ or produce spiritual fruit in our own power or ability. We need You not only for salvation, but to daily produce spiritual fruit in us and through us. Change us and make us living testimonies of Your transforming power. Please help us stay closely connected to You in prayer, in Your Word, in confession of sin, and in obedience. Fill us with Your Spirit daily and produce eternal fruit through our lives as we abide in You! Thank You for Your amazing grace. Amen.

DAY ONE

"I WAS READY TO DEFEND MYSELF. EXCEPT THIS TIME
I CAN'T. I HATE SAYING THIS. BUT I DESERVED TO GET
FIRED. I WAS DECEIVING THEM. I WAS DECEIVING YOU."
~TONY JORDAN, WAR ROOM

Confession is hard. It's admitting fault. Accepting guilt and responsibility. There is a step beyond confession, however—repentance. Tony's tone and the remainder of the film are an indication that his confession led to a total heart of repentance. Repentance is not only admitting sin, but also turning away from it. That is the divine work of God in our lives.

It is repentance that establishes forgiveness in our relationship with God. A believer can rightfully say that he is grateful for God's mercy regarding his sin. We may also say, "I am thankful for God's justice regarding my sin." That's less often said but just as much true. In God's justice, sin must be punished. In God's mercy, He provided Jesus to endure it. It would be unjust then to charge your sin against you since Christ already paid the price. Tim Keller writes regarding forgiveness in his book titled, *Prayer*: "It would be unjust for God to deny us forgiveness because Jesus earned our acceptance."[1]

There are two important keys to forgiveness.

The first key is atonement. Without the atonement of sin, there cannot be forgiveness.

READ 1 PETER 2:24 ABOUT ATONEMENT AND THE SACRIFICE JESUS MADE.

Whose sins did Jesus bear?

Jesus died so we might live for what?

How have you been healed?

What does it look like to live for righteousness in day-to-day life? How does your life reflect that?

The second key is repentance. Repentance is a beautiful and powerful thing.

What thoughts spring up when you see the word repentance? *Are they mostly negative? Positive? A little of both?*

READ ACTS 3:19 ABOUT REPENTANCE AND THE SOURCE OF FORGIVENESS.

Why do you need to repent and turn back?

What is the result of that repentance?

Who doesn't want seasons of refreshing in their life? If you feel like you're in a spot when you are not feeling a season of refreshing, perhaps you should seek repentance in an area of your life. Repentance is not a negative thing. Acts 3:19 clearly shows it leads to refreshment.

Get specific in repenting to the Lord. Do you need to repent in any of the following areas: pride, selfishness, control, or comparison or perfectionism?

Take some time to confess and repent in those areas. Ask God to help you to avoid these sins in the future. Consider telling your accountability partner. See how your life will change as a result of bringing your sins before the Lord in a specific way.

Use the remainder of your time today to compose your own prayer of repentance. To start, ask God to reveal to you areas of sin that you need to confess. Ask Him to change your heart's view of your sin so that you see it like God does. Wrong. Disgusting. Enslaving. Unnecessary. When you see your sin as God sees it, He will birth in you a desire to turn from it. Because of Christ's atoning sacrifice and your desire to repent, forgiveness is yours. His refreshing presence in your life can be more fully enjoyed. Close your prayer in silence reflecting on the sheer goodness of God in your life. Through His mercy, He gave Christ. Through His justice, the price was paid and your sin is forgiven. To God be the glory!

1. Timothy Keller, *Prayer* (New York, NY: Dutton, 2014), 209.

DAY TWO

"BUT I'VE LEARNED THAT MY CONTENTMENT CAN'T
COME FROM YOU. TONY, I LOVE YOU BUT I AM HIS
BEFORE I AM YOURS AND BECAUSE I LOVE JESUS, I AM
STAYING RIGHT HERE."

~ ELIZABETH JORDAN, WAR ROOM

START TODAY BY READING PHILIPPIANS 4:11-13.

The Greek word for *content* found in Philippians 4:11 is used only once in the Greek New Testament. Study that word below.

Content

Greek Word: Autarkes

Meaning: strong enough to need no aid or support; sufficient; independent of external circumstances; contented with one's lot, with one's means, though the slenderest.[1]

Contentment is an illusion in the American landscape today. The drive for more in every arena has created a culture where nothing is ever close to enough. More money. More status. More education. More busyness. More. More. More. Not necessarily all bad things, but the adage "too much of a good thing" certainly applies.

Where have you attempted to find contentment?

In what areas of life have you struggled to find contentment or to remain content?

Read Hebrews 13:5 and write it down in your own paraphrase in the space provided.

According to the writer of Hebrews, what promise from Jesus allows for contentment?

The nearness of Christ allows contentment regardless of circumstance. James writes to the dispersed believers in the early church, "Draw near to God, and He will draw near to you" (Jas. 4:8a).

When you find yourself plagued with discontentment how could drawing near to Jesus help you find contentment?

As Elizabeth's marriage was shattering, she learned to be content in Christ. The test of whether Christ is enough rarely happens when life is great. Your truest answer to the contentment question may come in your worst moments.

Name some difficult moments in your life when you felt the nearness of God. How did that bring contentment despite your circumstances?

Can you exude joy and remain content when the earth gives way underfoot? That's what Paul was saying. His response to imprisonment when writing to the church at Philippi was a message of contentment regardless of circumstances. Then came the famous quote in verse 13. "I am able to do all things through Him who strengthens me." Paul did not see contentment and comfort as synonymous. He knew he could be content even while being imprisoned for preaching the gospel. Why could Paul be so bold? Because he had learned the secret of contentment.

What things in this chapter helped Paul find contentment?

Philippians 4:6-7 -

Philippians 4:8 -

Philippians 4:9 -

Philippians 4:13 -

Philippians 4:19 -

Turn the things above into a prayer asking God to use these things to teach you to find your total contentment in Him regardless of your circumstances. Write your prayer and then pray it.

---

1. Thayer and Smith. "Greek Lexicon entry for Autarkes," *The KJV New Testament Greek Lexicon* [online] (cited 2 March 2015). Available from the Internet: *www.biblestudytools.com.*

DAY THREE

"I asked God to forgive me. But I need you to forgive me. I don't want you to quit on me, Liz."
~TONY JORDAN, WAR ROOM

"I forgive you."
~ ELIZABETH JORDAN, WAR ROOM

For your final personal Bible study, we present to you three of the most powerful words uttered in the film and an opportunity to read and reflect regarding their significance in your own life.

I. Forgive. You.

READ MARK 11:25.

What does this verse say we should do when praying?

READ HEBREWS 4:16.

What does this verse invite you to do?

In what manner does it invite you to do it?

In order to understand why we may approach God's throne so boldly, we need to look at the verses just prior.

GO BACK AND READ THE PREVIOUS CONTEXT FOUND IN HEBREWS 4:12-15.

From verses 12 and 13, we understand that the Word of God serves as a living judge, seeing and knowing all that everyone must give account for in his or her life. However, we are able to hold to a confession of faith because, via verses 14 and 15, we know that atonement has been achieved and sins have been forgiven by Jesus our High Priest. It is because of Christ's work of redemption that we might approach heaven confidently.

Without forgiveness, there can be no boldness, no confidence.

That is a change you see immediately in Tony.

Without forgiveness, there can be no generosity in relationships.

This is the change we have been waiting for in Elizabeth. Miss Clara explained earlier in the film that no one deserves God's grace. Now, content in Christ, Elizabeth knows that she belongs to Jesus before she belongs to Tony. That high view of God in her life enables her to extend forgiveness. It fosters a clear view of the gospel applied to life.

J.D. Greear explains that truly experiencing the gospel of Jesus means that no relationship is ever the same again. When presented with the challenge of being wronged or hurt, the gospel will remind you to look at yourself as sinner first and sinned against second. He writes that the "clearest mark of God's grace in your life is a generous spirit (think forgiveness) toward others."[1]

You may pray to God because you have been forgiven by God. You may offer that same forgiveness to others because it has first been given to you.

AS WE WRAP UP THIS STUDY, USE THE FOLLOWING QUESTIONS TO KEEP GROWING TOWARDS CHRISTLIKENESS.

How will you continue to examine your walk with Christ and seek to line it up with Scripture?

How will you help another believer grow in his or her walk with Christ?

How will you continue to lean on God's grace and submit to Him?

In what ways will you continue to resist the Devil?

Use the prayer of Miss Clara as your own.

HELP ME TO STAND ON YOUR WORD ABOVE ALL ELSE. HELP ME TO FIGHT ON MY KNEES AND WORSHIP YOU WITH MY WHOLE HEART. HELP ME TO PROCLAIM WITH MY LIFE THAT YOU ARE KING OF KINGS AND LORD OF LORDS. GUIDE ME TO PEOPLE WHO WILL CALL UPON YOUR NAME. RAISE UP THOSE WHO LOVE YOU AND SEEK YOU AND TRUST YOU. CALL US TO BATTLE, LORD.

1. J. D. Greear, *Gospel* (Nashville, TN: B&H Publishing, 2011), 120-121.

NOTES

NOTES